Somewhere Something is Burning

Alice Frecknall

Out-Spoken Press
London

Published by Out-Spoken Press,
Unit 39, Containerville
1 Emma Street
London, E2 9FP

A CIP record for this title is available from the British Library.

First edition published 2021
ISBN: 978-1-8380211-9-1

Typeset in Adobe Caslon
Design by Patricia Ferguson
Printed and bound by Print Resources

Out-Spoken Press is supported using public funding by the National
Lottery through Arts Council England and a grant from the Inclusive
Indies Fund administered by Spread the Word.

for Hannah and Rebecca

Contents

and passers-by see nothing but a little smoke

Vincent van Gogh

Crustacean

Google *anatomy of a crab*,
then *what is a compound eye*,
then *define cephalothorax*.
Think of a circle and a child
curled up at the centre, softly
fleshed, like a shell inside a shell.
Rampage the house, draw rings
around your mug, pen, mattress.
Undress, prod parts to check
they still move, scrawl *just not this!*
on a Post-it Note then circle
the words and stick it to the point
where, if you were ever opened
up, a heart would lie.

Broken GPS

I drop an anchor through the
floorboards thinking,

this must be the ocean; storm
the local football pitch

on team selection day, dressed
in all the right kit, waving

my arms and yelling, *PICK ME,
PICK ME, PICK ME*; glue

the emptied-out shells of a dozen
eggs back together and

pray to Customer Services that
more might come of them;

strap a kite to my ankles and
climb the cathedral; paint

myself head-to-toe, drive to
every gallery in the

county, a white plinth and a blurb
of tenuous links in the boot;

I learn balloon modelling from a
guy on the internet in

Mississippi; leave a sausage dog
and a wonky flower

stupidly close to a naked flame;
invite the neighbours

to a lineup of used cake wrappers,
a sign in Sharpie

on the back of an old chair, *LAST
CHANCE, EVERYTHING*

MUST GO; crawl into the airing
cupboard to fall asleep

among the stacks of clean towels,
the slow-to-ripen melons.

Paper

You said, I love you.

And I said, If you cut that right
you'll get paper snow.

And you said, I love you.

And I said, Babies don't have kneecaps and
outside a child is calling and I may be the
only one who has ears / the letters don't
know their postings and yet they go / we
put such pressure on the rain to be so
desperately wanted and hated, both / late
is actually early somewhere else / the wind
may be a bully to the clouds / I think the
leaves are in pain and so they moan / why
don't words realise what they are saying /
I only dream when I am sleeping.

And you said, I love you.

And I said, If you cut that right
you'll get paper houses.

And you said, I love you.

And I said, Adults are outliving their
kneecaps and inside a child is silent and I
may be the only one who has eyes / the
envelopes don't know what they are
hiding and yet stay sealed / we put such
pressure on the sun to be so desperately
exhausting and reviving, both / early is
actually late somewhere else / the clouds

may be a bully to the wind / I think the
leaves are tickled and so they laugh / why
don't words say what they realise / I only
sleep when I am dreaming.

And you said, I love you.

And I said, If you cut that right
you'll get paper people.

Best Kept Village

after Brigit Pegeen Kelly

Look! There's a nightingale standing on the patio with a hole where its beak should be. The homeowners are inside, busy Photoshopping a forlorn expression onto a poster, *Missing: songbird's beak (and song).*

The vicar has already been, of course. He turned up with multiple copies of *Mission Praise* and dragging an organ on casters, which he proceeded to strike with no real sense of rhythm, commanding, *Everybody now!* each time a chorus appeared.

A stop was put to it only when a piper passed, and the ivories all jumped ship. They went striding to the next village where, rumour has it, a baby's lost its laugh.

The baker arrives with leftover crumbs of pointless gestures, a hangnail from a thumbs-up, a lineless palm.

A lollipop lady leaves the world's children at the roadside to come and stand with two signs gaffer-taped back-to-back, *Go|Go* ringed encouragingly in green.

But the nightingale stands, head agape. Nothing.

The post woman tries her luck. *Perhaps more writer than public speaker*, she thinks, nudging a pen between the bird's talons. She places a carpet of letter paper at its feet. The pen slips from the nightingale's grip, draws a stuttering line, provokes a collective gasp. Morse code?

A local historian is brought in to translate: Dash. Dot. Dot. Dot. She paces before the bird for some time, muttering, *B... hmm... B... B...* until an abrupt stop startles all but the nightingale. *Aha!* she says, spearing the air with her index finger. *The BEES must have its beak!* And so the honey farmer comes next, professing the innocence of her colony.

The villagers bring out camping stoves, share tepid tins of Heinz, and bed down. They sleep in shifts, leaving an ear to hear the first chirp, a whistle, a decidedly tuneful breath. No.

At the first sign of the sun bleeding out, the nightingale cranes its neck, flicks a dewdrop from the tip of its wing.

The villagers stir just in time to catch sight of the bird taking flight, leaving them below, watching, mouths slack and empty as a hole.

Blue

Though I haven't yet
made it to death

I dress for my funeral
— all navy —

stand by a tightly made bed
and wait for the tide to come,

as a bluebottle
drives itself to madness

butting heads
with the outside.

Attachment Theory

Sound the alarm!
That's not a
squawking gull
but two tiny
human lungs
somewhere off
in the distance
scan the horizon
for a mother
on a Jet Ski
speeding waves
to rescue her babe
or a parachute
gliding into focus
from beyond thick cloud
the compass is crook
and each sob
locates North
in a different direction
then swings slack
maybe an escapee kite
with a fortuitously
low-hanging string
a friendly dolphin
to wrestle
into submission
lend a fin
make it stop!
The sky stares at
the mirrored sea and
that's my breakfast

overboard
cry SOS
to a shoal of tuna
only to discover they're
not the maternal type
referee a shouting match
between baby and thunder
count the seconds
from scream-to-scream
just to check
it's still breathing
before the next howl
rakes its poor throat
bellows the weather
into submission
and the sun sets itself up
for a cookout
thank goodness
this'll be it then
the sacred moment
when Mummy appears
and the whole thing
turns out to be
one huge mistake
like in a movie
on the news
just a misunderstanding
she only doubled
back to shore to
pick up a bottle
of Johnson's
this whole thing's
been blown out
of proportion

but she's here now
and raring for a tan
and yes of course
she loves her child
more than life itself
isn't that obvious
toasting flesh
back of the neck
with a beam
epiphany! Worse
someone get the kid
a tranquiliser
gummy bear
please God
the latest self-help book
a soundproof bunker
come on
you little urchin
can't you just
be reasonable?

Moving Day

When the house was sold, I left a piece
of myself in the cherry blossom, gave
a leg-up and told it to wait in case you
came back and needed a forwarding
address. The split felt like hunger, so I'd
eat until my ribs ached, hug my chest to try
and close the gap. Whenever the day is
yellow tint, I am still whole and seven, and
the tree out front is clustered with flowers,
half white, half pink; returning home with
my mother, the metal click of her key in the
yale like a miniature starting pistol, marking
the moment the ground turned light with
petals, branches a sudden silhouette.

Fruit Picking

She watches
the sallow
stream of pee,
crouched and
giggling, gags
herself when
a knock comes
and, *Girls?*
Wakes to held
breath and
screams, thin
walls making
everyone
complicit.
Twitching
curtains, flinch
of a fox.
Role-play. Static
shock at his
clothes against
hers, hers
against his. Jump
tyres to kerb,
the air riding
backie, hot
rubber and
green, ripe
clots on her
tongue, sweet
fingernails
muddy red.

Real Estate

She forces a raw smile up from her pillow, jokes she'll have bankrupted the Tooth Fairy, *I must remember to say sorry to the other children, Mummy.* Attempts to laugh, then teases a splinter from her gum before coughing up a summer. Grass, warm tarmac, the sunflower she measured growth against, all acid-bruised and drenched in bile, gush at the dam of her fingers, whilst her mother lifts her hair away.

With morning, the girl bares her jaws at the mirror hoping to see canines, incisors grinning at her. But instead, a white picket fence. Twenty-eight identical posts chiselled to perfect peaks.

The tests come through quicker than expected: 100% timber, a pine/spruce mix, soft but durable. *I'll book her in for a felling!* the dentist concludes. But a week after that, she's back in the chair.

Diverting to the hardware store, they pick out a stain, Cuprinol White Daisy. *Apply once a year, to protect against aging,* the shop assistant laughs as the girl pristines her slatted smile, watched by her mother who blinks a tear before it's ready to fall.

By Christmas, she hardly stumbles when the fence holds back, expects the weight hitting her gut, the ache, the absence in the air. And when her wisdom comes in, years later, it's no surprise to see four stone houses lining her mouth.

The new tenants are pleasant enough, with their weekly routine of mowing the buds from her tongue. And her mother arrives every third Wednesday to spend an afternoon lovingly pulling weeds from the gaps between where her molars should be, scattering respectable seeds as she goes. *Just wait for the Spring colours to bloom, dear.*

Holiday

Rubber ducks bob in the circular pool,
models of our family recipes on their backs.
A stuffed marrow capsizes into waterlog
and the chicken looks kind of anaemic.
The place seemed bigger online but
we don't mention it, having driven
through a heatwave to get here. A sign
points to a display of hanging bags,
Hook one to win. Inside each, a clenched
stomach like an embryo, smooth
and limbless, swings in the breeze.
Everything smells of chlorine and sweat,
and on the parched lawn a man hammers
hearts onto the posts of a coconut shy,
glistening muscle sticky on the turn. *Cheat!*
An indignant child brings out a notepad,
steadies their lens. I'm given a cotton wool
bullet, told it doesn't have to go all the way.
We pick at a pre-laid picnic of chewed
Nicorette, a strand of hair stuck to a
six-inch strip of electrical tape, *The Pocket
Guide to Dogs*, a doll, pillow-torso
stained, half-empty pack of Marlboro.
We make junk angels, sunbathe after dark.
The night tastes of raw meat and turps
and we swim laps, telling each other
we're all having such a wonderful time.

Heat

In thirty degrees on a beach,
a block of ice the height of
two fists protrudes from soft
sand. She kneels into the heat to
be close to it, slick thighs of
strangers pass, unacknowledging,
golden. A boy screams for
his fallen Cornetto, carries a
yolk-yellow spade, and a
gull has the devil in its eye.
Thumb and index okayed
around the base, she can feel
sun on her neck and no one
stops the push of her tongue,
plump as liver, pink tip extended,
tearing at the first frozen touch.

I go to sleep on my side of the bed.

Wake up on my side of the bed. Make coffee for three and spend the morning reheating. Cook enough food for a family. I wash my own dishes, romanticise my parents' old chest freezer. Leave the front door unlocked. Take the house key off the ring, examine its singular vulnerability. I draw my own face, over and over. Remove the pages from every book on the shelf. Leave negative reviews on the internet. Memorise the barcodes of my weekly shop. Spend £13.38. Refuse to day drink. Fetch, rollover, reward myself with tiny cubes of cheese. Order flowers to arrive on my doorstep. Adopt the fruit flies that flirt in my kitchen. Light too many candles, dip my finger where it isn't wanted. Talk to the windows about the weather, ask them if they feel it when the sun passes through.

Last Winter I Ate You Whole

The doctors said we were lucky,
the retrieval a complete success.
Left alone in the recovery room, I
pestered a junior for a toothpick
and levered the remnants from
my molars, placed your best side
in a Tupperware just out of reach.
Today I had a breakthrough,
spent all afternoon colour-coding
the fridge, alphabetising the
spice rack, whilst a baked apple
sat on the counter marinating
in a memory — that house on the
cliff with the bowed roof and
good wine. A squeeze of lime
and I think everything should
balance out quite nicely. I've been
studying the science, learning
how much of you is safe to
swallow. But I don't yet trust it,
often find myself pacing through
the night, adrift in the dark, unfed.

Love Letter

Seven magpies tap at the window
and a frenzied grandmother
starts whistling. A kicking baby
lies flat on its back, and a miniature
tortoise keeps crawling into my shoes.
A snake mimics yesterday's belt,
an undone spiral on the carpet.
There's a feather in my throat,
taste of blood from a missing wing,
the sharp catch of broken quills.
In the drawer, a heap of dead leaves
and a looking glass reflecting
a cloudless white sky. My pockets
are stuffed with autumn. On the TV,
a black and white time-lapse of
my first thirty years, in which the
character of me is played by a stranger
and I cameo as Friend Number Two.
The back of my head becomes a trope
only my hairdresser and my mother
would recognise. Credits roll my name
on repeat, then nothing, a slight hum
and a blank screen, carries on
scrolling until I take a hammer to it
and a single magpie flies
from the shards, fractures
into flame, air smoking.

Tulips

The tulips have grown half an inch
since you went. Gangling teenagers
cut off at the foot and plunged.

They are in denial, they go on
craning their necks towards the gods.

Don't judge me, but I've taken to leaving
the lights on when I sleep, afraid I'll stumble
over their outsized bodies in the night.

Mother Married a Rock

Their first night in matrimony
she carved her initials into its face,
hunting blood in a scrabble for passion,
blew the dust from its veins, choking,
and declared the act finished before
it began. Lying beside her love,
contrails taunted her with thoughts
of strangers carried over thresholds,
aircrafts of people strapped at the waist.
Had they looked at just that moment
and seen her bride? A magnificence
of off-white punctuating the landscape.
That colour, a tease playing catch
with the sun, how it threw back the light
and turned shadows into ghosts that
danced as only human bodies can.

Weekend Getaway

We fold back the cover to find ourselves
at sea in a plot of unfathomable length.
Trapped in the ceiling light, a fly
names our first born, refuses to grant us
visitation rights. A fountain is pissing
full-bodied relief outside the window
and a seagull screams for breakfast.
Yesterday's clothes feel like a costume.
Open the suitcase and nothing,
a seasoning of salt, and sand, and talc.
Rain. Tilt your head back, say *ahh*.
Your tongue a shrivelled bud. We take
bets on a storm, a sunset. Take a walk
to the beach, along the shingle, pause
in the shallows, toes kissing beneath
the water as we face each other, hijack
a fishing boat, reel in a net of flailing limbs.

I Ask the Flowers

to please me, by the window
to attention in a narrow vase.

Take one stem — lay it
bloom to pillow.

Awake and asleep and awake
again, miss the moment

but come morning, petals are shed,
there's pollen in my eye.

My thigh is a fistful of bruise,
dress but do not wash.

Clutch coffee,
mouth to ash, sipping

in the doorway, watching
its form, narrow as a little boy's.

See Figure 1.
after Ocean Vuong

After our diagnosis, *this is over*, I held
    a ritual and ate the watch off my wrist.

Note to self:
    leather is nothing like beef jerky.

Summer is threatening to come again.

My grandparents planted an oak tree
in their garden the summer they
    were first married.

I sit out afternoons in the living room,
silences stacking up the chimney, fire raging
    despite the season.

Smoke thickens, brings short-sightedness.

7.02am: my cough is back.

Ill or tired?

I woke to find it on my pillow smirking
    through the dark, just waiting.

There is a tapping. I think it is coming from
    outside, not from within me.

No matter.

Note to self: second-hand smoke
    contains 7,000 chemicals. Plus.

On average, you'll lose 10 years to
    perfectly rolled cigs.

Are my insides a fog yet?

There is no violence in death. Not naturally.
Only a quiet tussle into nothing.

8.37am: woodpecker or DIY?

My grandmother said, *I only dated him
for his car, you know.*

A Morris Garages classic. A catch.

Memory is a deadweight. It does not sleep.

It lies on your side of the bed and counts
down to another day like any other,
heated porridge oats and milk.

In the winter of 2009 you left the espresso
maker on the stove, unwatched.

I could smell the fumes in your nostrils
for weeks each time we spoke too close.

10.21am: my stomach is roaring.

I watched two scientists on the news cut
open a dead seabird to reveal
its stomach a mesh.

Over 200 bits of discarded plastic.

Nature cannot be trusted with itself.

Last night I dreamt your lover sliced me
open, removed my stomach and placed it
in a locked box made from oak,

threw away the key, not yet ready to know
all the things I have consumed.

My grandmother said, *your grandfather
sold his car to pay for the wedding.*

But by then, there was nothing either
could have done.

The Adult Authentication Centre

Try this one for size,
just below the nose.

Stretch the corners up a touch,
not to the point of frenzied but
enough to have something convincingly
cheerful for your photo pass.

How do you feel about orange?

Second thoughts, best not.
Something bright though. Lime green?

Pink?
Fuchsia!

No? A backdrop then.
The Happy Family series is quite popular
with your age bracket.

I'm afraid not. The small print's there,
see? *Not included.*

Next to the clause about
pet allergies. Never mind…

High-Flying Couple?

Oh! Here,
the Strong Independent range. You're lucky,
we've quite a number of these left in stock.

I'll just need copies of your
mortgage agreement, full-time salary,
pension plan, and net worth

of any investments.
What's that?

Right.
Yes, I do understand.

Actually,

could I ask you
to step aside?

There's an exit ahead of you there,
between the Fairy-Tale Bundles and
the Blissful Retirements.

Don't worry, it's not that you've
done anything wrong. I mean,
it doesn't make a difference to me
but it's a matter of sensitivity.

Don't want to make the others feel
uncomfortable, do we? Bad for business.

No don't be silly, love,
you can keep the smile.

We can't reuse them anyway,
health and safety.

**Please Note: single diners
may have to share a table at busy times**

The waiter removes my coat and, folding
it over his arm, smooths the breath out of it.

Cyanosis

My landlord forbids
the use of Blu Tack
but drilling is fine.
At the dentist's I refuse
to sign the papers, break
into the reception stationery
and repair my cracked molar
with a pea-sized ball of putty.
I refuse to marry. A doctor
stands me heels-to-wall
and colour-matches
my height to steel.
He cites the cold tinge,
a lack of oxygen, a clear
malfunction of the heart.
I walk to get away
from myself.
I can go for hours,
watch the sun as it places
its lips softly on rooftops
then slips away.
For sixty seconds
the heath is a flood of ink.
Each morning,
I pull my blinds more
slowly in case the sky has fallen.
I catch the bluebells
quite by accident, take a turn
and there they are.
I pick a bunch,
lick my fingers

to keep the moment.
The next person I kiss
will taste unexpected
bitterness, a wilted petal,
something pissy.
A mother drags
her screaming toddler
from the lake, which
delivers it newborn again.
I try to recall the exact shade
of a stranger's eyes, settle
on sapphire though
I know it impossible.
Heat helps a blueberry
live up to its name;
run the tap and watch
as a punnet turns Prussian.
I look at art,
stand in Tate Modern
and lose myself
in Klein's rectangle,
weigh-up swatches in B&Q
then head home to paint
my portrait, walls, ceiling.
My grandmother tells me
'sludge' is more my palette.
At dinner, she comments
on the décor, asks
if I have friends.
Smiling, I pretend
not to hear and offer
her more greens.

She is lying

in bed thinking about
the hand of God, a
giant full-faced thumb
bearing down,
crevices of skin like
rivers, descending
so slowly, quietly, she
hardly notices, doesn't
move. A burst blood vessel
like a squashed insect
disrupts the arc of the life
line and, next to it, fate
is clearly visible. *Of all
the things God shouldn't
need*, she thinks. There's
something earthy,
salt and soap, a complex
web of veins channelling
to the surface. The
floor becomes a lake
rising around her, palm
a canopy of gentle
warmth now so close to
the chilled tip of
her nose. Her head
is forced back,
water lapping
at the sides of the
mattress, sodden sheets.
It finds her, gathers
in the scar of her

navel. She pushes
against flesh, chokes
on the stagnant swill as
she's plunged and
held through the sound
of her ribs cracking
like knuckles, one
after the other, then
released gasping,
completely unmoved.
Above her, splintered
slats of a top bunk,
a sister's heavy breaths.

Take These, They're Falling!

An armful of babies, bare
rabbit hinds ready to bolt,
their hair dark as mine, each
a matching birthmark, eyes
green/brown and too big.
Warm bodies slip, piss running
down forearm. *Be careful!*
A woman wearing my face
gathers saliva-slick fingers.
They're falling! Damp thud of a
skull, bloody smear at my
feet and in my fist a foot, toes
splayed and tiny, and I hold it
so tightly so tightly so tightly.

Magic Trick

To test the magician's skills, she straps
him in a straitjacket, binds him with
chains, and swallows. The penny-slot-drop
of her oesophagus takes and rejects, his
feet, knees hit her stomach, teeter,
crescendo. She forgets to breathe,
half-expecting him to clatter right out,
then smirks into the silence, strokes
the rounding of her middle. *You are
so loved*, she whispers. *I'll keep great care
of you.* Inviting herself to the show, she
signs her name in black with crimson
accents, leaves it smudged on her pillow
then grins as she reads it. The excitement
swarms before the covers lift on her belly
to rapturous applause, flesh rippling
as he squirms and lashes against his
ties. He strangles to speak. The oxygen
dancing waltz from his lips forms a
hiccup of a word, stretches her jaw
with sound like whale-speak. Heaving
in prayer at the toilet bowl, she gags
against the ache breeding from her core
as fragments of conversation snake
strings of spew. *He has managed it!* she
thinks. Face wet, she spits. Calm, before
the next surge threatens. She chokes,
hurls a punch, and with a final writhe his
last frustration roars. The body still, she

takes a fishing line, a rusting finger-hook
to summon him out, forces it down,
makes the catch. She tugs through the
ripping drag. Pulling at the cut of her
waistband, she swears she can feel a beat
out of sync, a heart, a phantom kick.

Easter Sunday

On Ash Wednesday a ghost moved in
and every day after a brick has fallen from
the house, bringing a fresh landslide of
rubble. I've been buried twice already,
to the ankle then mid-shin. It's bad for
the lungs so I hold my breath. The utility
bills have rocketed. Three showers a day,
water sits on my skin like little glass
paperweights. I try to reason but every
argument incites another flurry of plaster
and the neighbours come knocking
about noise. This time of year is always
surprising. Now a heatwave, once sixteen
and thick snow, and yet still the daffodils
are wild and happy. A woman collapses
at the communion altar in the name of
love and I envy the lambs, chosen and
defrosted overnight, readied for a feast.

Plateau

it's been thirty-plus years
standing by a sink
                squeezing a tea bag
against the side of a mug   the
drip
                  cutting a cake
counting flames in neat rings
         each hour falling off the
                    clock face
into a single slow clap
a folded tissue
        the continuous deciding
            whether to or not
blood puckering at seam of skin
        pressured thumb on wrist
holding joy   rusted blades
             in perfect threes
getting good news in public
with only the grass to tell
    noticing the exact peach-pink
              of the light
pointing, *look — a rainbow!*
smiling to a stranger's cockapoo
kicking a cat
          measuring the length
    of each white hair   a sharp
              pluck
a knot
      tied around an index finger
the perpetual wondering
at what's being forgotten

         parents fading
a documentary
on freezing human eggs
those untold things
           curved flanks
a boy saying, *I want to*
a man
      the sound of static before
                thunder
        woman   sweat
running
toes poised
        a sentence breaking
forty-plus years
standing by a sink
         squeezing a tea bag
against the side of a mug   the
drip
          cutting a cake
counting flames in neat rings

Preface

You forget the words to the prayer, exit
the church to find God riding shotgun
along the B1040, teen sweetheart at the
wheel, roadkill in their wake; imprint of
a tyre tread like a family crest in a pool
of sealing wax, a splinter of bone strangely
clean. There's a ticking from your naked
wrist. Around you, a yard of stone doors,
someone's knocking. Go from carved
handle to carved handle until one
of them gives. A small wooden statue,
carpenter's join visible at the waist. You
pull it apart to find a replica of your sister
nestled inside, again and the next, your
childhood best friend, your mother, father,
you; height of a pen lid, smile no more
than a hyphen between rose-painted
cheeks. You split, spill a torso of ash, and
the vicar is there, falling to his knees,
working your remains into the ground.

Writing to You

Each letter, the
purest origami — a
blank sheet folded
like a book, sealed
and stamped. Months
stack and yellow.
Top of the pile, ringed
twice with coffee,
you are held in the eye
of a Venn diagram.
To the open-mouthed
red box, touch cold lip
and back, still clutching
paper inside an
unseasonable jacket.

Welcome to Departures

The floors have all turned to tar

so she does not move from the chair
that cradles her backside like a mother's lap.

Time curves in her palm, a limp claw,
as she waits for the walls to speak.

And in the time it's taken time
to form a perfect 'C', a butterfly

has made its way about the place
searching for something.

It pauses at the window, blinks a wing,
daring the universe to break.

How cruel of the world to show up like this.

With the seductiveness of an autumn
that hasn't yet come

and cannot be smelled from here.

She looks from the glare of it back
to the sombre pool swelling the room.

Dips a toe.

Inside her chest is a sting.

The image he showed her was whiteout
on black. It too was curved,

his vertebrae slotting together in an arc
resembling a wasp's abdomen, and

amongst the chevrons of bone, a dark dot

as if God had stubbed out a cigarette
and accidently set something else burning.

Stockpiling

Under my pillow: a wooden fork
and a squirming tooth, wingspan of a kite
and the scent of salted sky and orange.

Before you go, tell me again about how
to keep paint alive, and I promise not to say,
I know this — about the spray bottle
and fine, quenching mist.

There are laughter lines in every pair
of your shoes. Stepping aboard the toecaps,
I hug air in want of your waist and wait
for them to lead me in a staggering dance.

One item at a time the furniture turns into
paper cut-outs — the dining table pasted in
from an IKEA catalogue, floorboards
a repurposed advertisement for fencing.

The pictures have regressed to commercial
shots of unbelievably happy people
and there's something off with the windows.

See how the weather comes right in?
An assembly of trees, grass, ants, birds;
a robin, chest military; a rabbit scrabbling
at the door, claws scoring the painted
wood, keeping count.

And me, a child in a hand-me-down
swimming costume, learning to dive by
throwing a brick and watching as it sinks.

The Vault

Into the desert of a hallway, three feet
above where the carpet once was, top of a
cupboard, a shelf now undulating dunes,
staircase a cliff. There's sand in my turn-ups,
filling the eyelets of my shoes. A pebble,
soft grey, impossibly smooth, pale line
meandering like a vein on the inner side
of a forearm. I am delicate as a parent
reaching into a pram to touch a child's
cheek knowing it is beautiful. Next to it,
a disconnected phone, screen a black hole.
The stitches of my pocket strain to take it
and on the ground a spiral shell. Held to
my ear, a hundred voices close enough
to kiss fall over themselves to be heard.

The Signs

An orchid gives birth
to a white bud, another
and another, each withering
before the next, and a squirrel
falls to its death at our feet,
corpse a kiss in the dirt,
tail resting along its back
like an exploded spine.
I turn its coat into a mitten,
score a penknife along its throat,
beneath its little armpits; bring
its fur to my cheek, soothing.
A sunlit clearing frames
a bench with a blank
inscription, disembodied
voice of an out-of-tune choir.
We join for a round of
Never have I ever and end
up on a ward, kidneys fried.
The ants weep at the machines
falling silent, and a hare
takes you by the hand.
Trusting the twitch of its nose,
veins itching, you go — toughened
skin of your fingers, a burn
on the roof of my mouth.
The sky pays tribute;
paints our portrait,
equal parts air and water,

the likeness uncanny.
A dove catches its wing
in my teeth, hangs snapped
and angular, its downy chest
beating against my chin:
enough— enough— enough—

Acknowledgements

I would like to thank the editors at *Butcher's Dog* magazine, in which an earlier version of 'Crustacean' was first published.

An earlier version of 'Real Estate' was shortlisted under a different title for the Out-Spoken Prize for Poetry 2019, and published online by Out-Spoken; my thanks to the judges and staff.

This book was made possible thanks to an Arts Council National Lottery Project Grant.

Thanks

I extend huge thanks to my editor, Joelle Taylor, for taking a chance and believing in this book when it was barely a seed. For all your encouragement, enthusiasm, trust, and reassurance. Without you, it would not exist as it does.

To Out-Spoken Press for giving my poems such a wonderfully caring home. To Patricia Ferguson for all your patience and incredible hard work in bringing this book into the physical world.

Special thanks to Caroline Bird for coming on this journey with me. For your wisdom, understanding, honesty, and intuition, and for always pushing me to take more risk. Your mentorship has been so important, and your work is ever inspiring.

To Tom MacAndrew for helping me secure funding to support the writing of this book. Thank you for being a friend through this process, for answering my endless questions, and for always checking in.

Heartfelt thanks to Arts Council England for funding the time needed to write this book and enabling me to develop and work as an artist.

To laura jane lee, lisa luxx, Safiya Kamaria Kinshasa, and Sarah Fletcher for sharing in this experience. For your poetry, guidance, and generosity of spirit.

To UniSlam and the Post-Emerging Cohort, with particular thanks to Toby Campion and the Wednesday night Zoom crew: Bryony Littlefair, Cecilia Knapp, Elisabeth Sennitt Clough, Jemima Foxtrot, Maria Ferguson, Shruti Chauhan, and Talia Randall. Your feedback and camaraderie throughout the strangest of years has been invaluable.

To Apples and Snakes for your ongoing support, and for enabling me to attend the Arvon writing retreat where I first found the voice that belongs to this book. And to Arvon for the nurturing environment that helped me to begin.

To Suzi Corker for nudging me to press 'send' on the email that eventually led to all this, and for being the most generous (and the best) photographer I have the privilege to know.

To James Smart for your feedback, time, and insightful questioning at various stages of the writing process.

To my sister and friend, Rebecca Frecknall, for your considered advice and feedback, for keeping me going, and never doubting my work would get here.

Finally, and always, thank you to my family and my friends for your unwavering love and support.

Other titles by Out-Spoken Press